To My Beautiful
Great Grandson
the I Love
" Liam "

SLEEP TIGHT NASHVILLE

written by DAVE DIETRICH and DEBBIE BROWN

illustrated by KATHRYN GOGLIOTTI

We're off to bed, Nashville,
we must say goodnight.

From Broadway to Opry, we
hope you sleep tight!

Sleep tight
famous singers
with names etched
in red stars.

Sleep tight Science Center where I blast off to Mars!

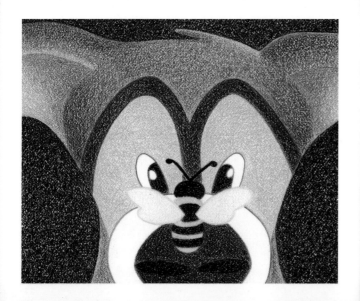

Sleep tight Second Avenue

with your bright lights and shops.

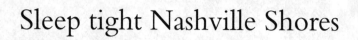
Sleep tight Nashville Shores

where I do BELLY FLOPS!

Sleep tight Cumberland River where boats glide along.

Sleep tight "Batman Building,"
you are so very tall.

Sleep tight Opryland Hotel
and Opry Mills Mall.

Sleep tight Pancake Pantry
so delicious and sweet.

Sleep tight Loveless Café
with fluffy biscuits to eat.

Sleep tight Parthenon in Centennial Park

and the Dog Day Festival where lots of dogs bark.

Sleep tight baseball
stadium with your
guitar scoreboard.

Sleep tight
all you Titans

and Predators too.
No other fans cheer as loud as we do!

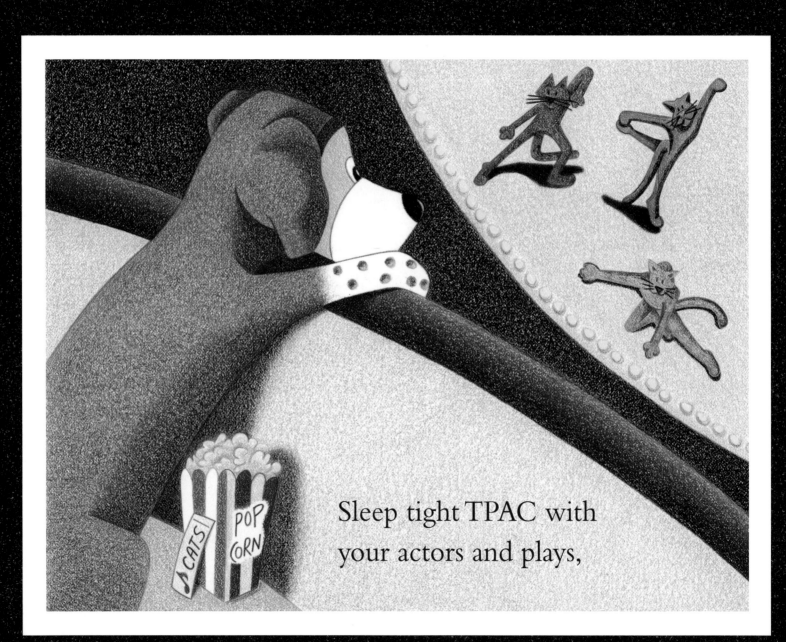

Sleep tight TPAC with
your actors and plays,

Festivals and concerts
on warm summer days.

Sleep tight
Nashville Zoo

where the
animals roam.

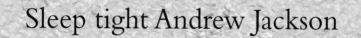

Sleep tight Andrew Jackson

in your Hermitage home.

Sleep tight Nashville
and sleep tight my dear.

Sleep tight Music City,
ya'll come back now, ya hear!

Sleep Tight Nashville Fun Facts

Nashville, TN
Our city was founded on Christmas Eve in 1779.

Grand Ole Opry®
The original name of this famous country music show was the WSM Barn Dance.

Adventure Science Center™
The sun is almost 93 million miles away from this place and the queen bee lays up to 2,000 eggs a day!

Second Avenue and Broadway
Ride a bike, see a hockey game, shoot lasers, eat barbecue, shop for boots…just some of the things you can do in the heart of downtown Nashville.

Music City Walk of Fame
Started in 2006, inductees include Reba McEntire, Kid Rock, Elvis, and Les Paul.

Nashville Shores™
This park has eight water slides, a wave pool, and a lazy river that require about one million gallons of water!

RCA Studio B™
There are still red, blue, and green lights in this music studio from when Elvis recorded his Christmas album here.

Sounds Baseball
In 2015, our favorite minor league team won their first game in the new stadium 3-2…in extra innings.

The Batman Building
The "Batman Building" is 617 feet to the top – currently the tallest building in Tennessee!

Gaylord Opryland Resort and Convention Center®
This resort contains nine acres of gardens and a 44-foot cascading waterfall!

Opry Mills Mall®
This used to be the Opryland USA theme park, but is now Tennessee's largest shopping outlet.

Pancake Pantry™
Did you know you can eat more than 20 types of pancakes here?!

Loveless Cafe™
They serve up what many have referred to as "the best biscuits in America."

The Parthenon
It's the only full-scale replica of the original Parthenon from Athens, Greece.

Cumberland River
This river winds its way through 688 miles of Tennessee and Kentucky.

Dog Day Festival
You could see more than 5,000 furry friends at this event which supports the Humane Association.

Ryman Auditorium®
A riverboat captain named Thomas Ryman built this historic music venue more than 100 years ago.

Titans Football
We love our football in Nashville, especially magical moments like the 75-yard touchdown play in 2000 famously called the "Music City Miracle."

Nashville Predators™
The skeleton of a saber-toothed cat was once found in downtown Nashville and that's how the Predators got their mascot.

The Hermitage
The driveway of this home of our 7th U.S. President, Andrew Jackson, is in the shape of a guitar.

Nashville Zoo at Grassmere™
Our zoo is home to the Jungle Gym: the largest community-built playground in the country!

Tennessee Performing Arts Center (TPAC)
TPAC is home to opera, ballet, and lots of plays. Did you know it can take 90 hours to make a professional tutu?!

Live Music
Nashville is home to LOTS of concerts and events like the CMA Music Festival which takes place over four days and features more than 400 artists.

ACKNOWLEDGEMENTS

This book is dedicated to the city of Nashville and to kids of all ages who are each blessed with unique and wonderful talents. We hope you fully embrace the thrill of reading books and allow your creativity to flourish no matter what life throws your way.

Special thanks to the following people for going above and beyond to support this book:

Fred and Bev Lyttle
Jason Dietrich
Andrea Leljak
Kathryn Gogliotti
Megan and Isla Dietrich
Bandit and Ace
Matt and Mary Washburn
Nashville Predators
Larry Brown

Sleep Tight Nashville
First Edition – October, 2016

ISBN 13: 978-0-692-49949-8

www.sleeptightnashville.com

Printed by PRC Book Printing 400 Lincoln Ave, Hatboro, PA 19040, USA.

A portion of all profits will support the PENCIL Foundation of Nashville
www.pencilfoundation.org

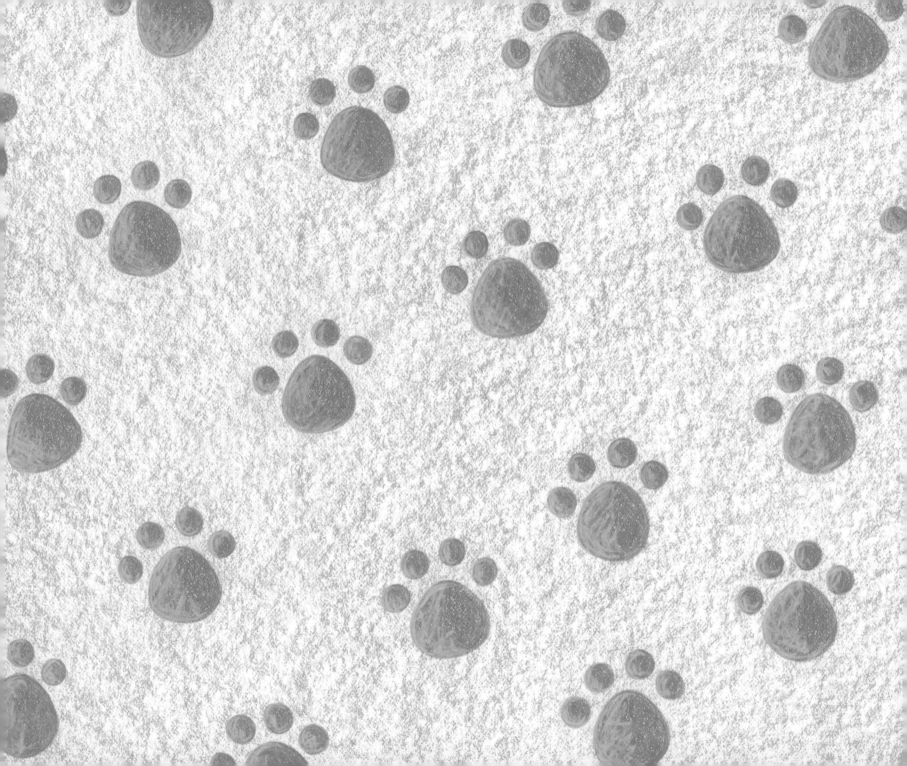